My Bi-Polar MamaBear

T.A. Mystic

WWW.TEHOMCENTER.ORG

My Bi-Polar MamaBear
ISBN: 978-1-960326-64-5
Copyright © 2024 by T.A. Mystic

Tehom Center Publishing is a 501c3 non-profit imprint of Parson's Porch Books. Tehom Center Publishing celebrates feminist and queer authors, with a commitment that at least half our authors are people of color. Its face and voice is Rev. Dr. Angela Yarber.

Dedication

For my daughter, Chania, "the girl," you are more than a diagnosis code or the world's stigma. Thank you for allowing us to care for Nirvana Skye, for it was truly the greatest act of compassion and trust. We see you, we accept you, and we will always love you.

To Nirvana Skye, you are my favorite person in the world, and it is an honor to be your "Ya-Ya."

My Bi-Polar MamaBear wears different hats that tell me how she will feel and act.

I am her daughter SkyeBear, and I am the only one with the power to see her like that.

Sometimes she walks and talks very, very fast, even faster than me.

That's because she is wearing the yellow hat for extreme energy.

I miss her so much since I can't see her every day.

So, I imagine her wearing the purple hat that keeps her safe along the way.

Today it's a blue hat; she is sad and crying a whole lot.

I give her many hugs and kisses; she is loved more than she thought.

My Uncle CamBear tells me, "MamaBear's brain makes her think and act differently than you and me."

He says, "She has big people problems, and it is never your fault." His explanation helps me see.

Oh no!! It's the black hat! She is now screaming mad, which scares me so.

Thankfully my Gi-GiBear covers my eyes and ears and politely asks her to go.

Many days and nights go by
before the black hat falls off and
MamaBear visits us again.

Then when she returns, we
welcome her with open arms and
the fun times begin.

Yay!!! She is wearing my favorite rainbow hat! She reads to me, and we sing funny songs.

We play and eat together, but that hat doesn't stay on for very long.

Bye-Bye, SkyeBear.

Bye-Bye, my Bi-Polar MamaBear, I hope to see you again one day soon.

I'll dream of you wearing your red hat, so you'll remember that I love you more than the space between the ocean and the moon.

A Note to Adult Readers and Educators

Approximately 1.6 million adults in the U.S. live with bipolar disorder and a third of those suffer from substance abuse addictions; these diseases display similar symptoms and consequences. My daughter is among this number, and as a result, became incapable of providing a stable environment to care for my granddaughter. I decided to create a way to explain and educate Nirvana Skye so she could understand her mom's behaviors are "big people" problems, and more importantly, to remind her that these circumstances are not her fault. Notably, the colors of the hats and dresses are matching to signify how this illness, specifically the mood changes, impact the child.

The term "bipolar" remains taboo, as a result of society simply labeling it as an excuse for a simple mood fluctuation or, worse, labeling people as crazy and manic. These inappropriate and minimizing usages demoralize, stigmatize, and isolate those who are suffering from bipolar disorder. There are numerous children who have been displaced, transitioned into new families, or currently still reside with or know someone who displays the behaviors presented in this book.

Unfortunately, today's world provides limited resources to educate and support this growing population, thereby hindering the development of coping methods required to enhance the healing processes for all who are affected.

My hope is that this book will promote open-ended, educational conversations with children that will allow them an outlet to express their feelings. Additionally, this simple book may assist parents, caregivers, and others who don't understand bipolar disorder. My wish for everyone is to gain the ability to spread universal tolerance, support, and understanding for individuals suffering from these debilitating diseases.

Tehom Center Publishing is an imprint publishing feminist and queer authors, with a commitment to elevating BIPOC writers. Amplifying authors from the margins bent on writing toward justice is our calling and joy.

In addition to traditional, independent publishing at no cost to the author, Tehom Center Publishing also offers one-on-one and group coaching that empowers authors in book writing, book marketing, and book entrepreneurship through an intersectionally feminist lens.

Learn more at www.tehomcenter.org/tehom-center-publishing